Picking the Lovely

Poems by
Griggori Tyler Taylor

;or

The Gospel of Listening

Magic by
Eldinazi Lycrii Vahnterri

Copyright © 2013 by Griggori Tyler Taylor
All rights reserved. This book or any portion thereof may not be reproduced or used in any manner whatsoever without the express written permission of the publisher except for the use of brief quotations in a book review or blog.

Original cover art by Toney Little
Modifications by Victoria Caldwell and CoverDesignStudio.com

Printed in the United States of America First Printing, 2013
ISBN 978-0615919232

River City Poetry Paducah, KY 42001

Ordering Information:
Quantity sales. Special discounts are available on quantity purchases by corporations, associations, and others. For details, contact the publisher by email. Orders by U.S. trade bookstores and wholesalers. Please contact Big Distribution: via email

www.rivercitypoetry.com

scribble-toys.tumblr.com

griggori.taylor@gmail.com

For the Song-healers

If you have the kind of eyes that see,
I hid a lot of Magic in this book.
Use it well.

There is some confusion as to what magic actually is. I think this can be cleared up if you just look at the very earliest descriptions of magic. Magic in its earliest form is often referred to as "the art". I believe this is completely literal [...]   Art is, like magic, the science of manipulating symbols, words, or images, to achieve changes in consciousness.

At the moment the people who are using Shamanism and magic to shape our culture are advertisers.   Rather than try to wake people up, their Shamanism is used as an opiate to tranquilize people, to make people more manipulable. Their magic box of television, and by their magic words, their jingles can cause everyone in the country to be thinking the same words and have the same banal thoughts all at exactly the same moment.

In latter times I think that artists and writers have allowed themselves to be sold down the river. They have accepted the prevailing belief that art and writing are merely forms of entertainment. They're not seen as transformative forces that can change a human being; that can change a society.

-Alan Moore

An old joke puts its thus, "when a man speaks to a god it's prayer, when a god speaks to a man it's schizophrenia"... Many people hear voices without suffering any of the debilitating and dysfunctional effects associated with schizophrenia, some treat these as sources of inspiration or develop religious ideas around them, others become mediums or occultists.

Magic is the science and the art of causing change to occur in conformity with will.

Man considers himself a center of will and a center of perception. Will and perception are not separate but only appear as so to the mind. The unity which appears to the mind to exert twin functions of will and perception is called Kia by magicians. Sometimes it is called the spirit, or soul, or life force, instead.

-Peter Carroll

This is a time when people are choosing sides…

-Paris Shortridge

Picking the Lovely

The first book of Eldinazi

CONTENTS

Acknowledgments
Forward

Part one: A Dinner of Dreamcraft in the Blood
       1. The Catacombs are Breaking
       2. Beyond the In-between
       3. The Kiteflyer
       4. Pocket Words
       5. Two Moons
       6. Figure Drawing
       7. Prayer for Bohemia
       8. To Those Who don't Meet
       9. Absconditus
       10. Whisperhenge
       11. The Second Crash
       12. The Kites Inside your Chest
       13. For My Father, Catcher of the Bigger Fish
       14. The Mini Revolt
       15. Nine Days
       16. Dandelions

*

Part two: A Museum of Muse in the Heart
       16. Heading Home
       17. A Rib & A Smile
       18. If You weren't What You Are
       19. Two Cups
       20. Three Triangles
       21. Easter Eggs
       22. Alert
       23. A Quiltstitch Waltz
       24. Chantepleure
       25. The Orange
       26. The New Exhibit
       27. Letter to Stranger
       28. Concretes
       29. Ledger Lines
       30. Contained

*

Part three: A Picturehouse of Promise in the Skull
        31.   Anatomy
        32.   Thoughts While Watching a Dying Star
        33.   Every Curve, Line, and Angle
        34.   Them Birds
        35.   Fire
        36.   Fly
        37.   Armor
        38.   Small Talk
        39.   You Should Let
        40.   Abstracts
        41.   Un-anchor the Angels
        42.   Thoughts While Cooking Red-beans & Rice

*

About the Author

Acknowledgments

To the song-healers.

To the ones who realize they are made in the image of God. To the ones who become humans instead of consumers. To the ones who choose scripture instead of dogma. To the ones who discovered God is too big for one book. To the ones who hum to tree rings. To the ones who read the rain. To the ones who are strong enough to let it go. To the ones who left their hate behind for we know not the battles weighing on another's shoulders. To the ones who care not what other think of them because it is none of their business. To the ones who deny judgment. To the disturbers of mindless peace. To the meek who help the meek. To the ones who care more about what is written on paper than how much paper they have. To the ones who know the real world is fake. To the ones who carry on. To the ones who put the picture together. To the ones who realized Fox News is full of shit. To the ones who find their own truth. To the New Age. To the global consciousness. To the energy movers. To the light workers. To the Christians who sold everything they owned and gave it to the poor. To the lovers. To the Bohos and the Hobos. To the Shamans. To the Wizards. To the Mystics. To the ones who know we are one. Much love to you all.

To the writers who stitched inspiration to my truest self. To Niaz Khadem, for sowing the words of the poet I would become. Without you there would have been no ground to work with, and I would have most likely given up on poetry by now. To Pat Stafford, for being my bridge to the classic view of this craft, and for being the strongest editor and critic of my work. You are the greatest poet I know. I long to read your books. To Gabriel Camacho, a walking revolution, forerunner of the river city poets, a man who makes things happen. To Levi McDuffee, the future, the new wave, receiver of the torch that caused the inferno. To Matt Curtis, my brother in arms, the one who opened the doors, the one who kept me going. I wish to drift across this country with you again. To Grace Yocum, heart-thief, a voice for the new age. To Jacob Gipson, SNES, the next generation. To Samuel Hawkins, the poet who set fire to the mic. every night, the dream-weaver, the one who made making it a reality. I hope to keep writing and performing with you, in this life and the next. Much love to you all.

To the Saints in my life's Chapel. To Bro. Jeff Cruse, for taping in to the phone-line of God and helping me do the same. Your sermon on callings changed my life forever and put me on the path I needed. If you find yourself owning a copy of this book, I hope that you enjoy it more than you worry. Sins against civilized society and sins against God, I have found, are rarely the same thing. We are on the same side, regardless of what they may say. God bless. To Bobby Collins, for teaching me the lost arts and showing me how to speak to the plants and the stars. I hope the spirits are with you as they are with me. To Paris Shortridge, for being my primary provider of light in times of darkness, for helping me start what I was created to do. Much love to you all.

To my Blood. To my Father, provider, for giving me what I needed to progress through times of heaviness, for allowing me the freedom to tinker with the parts of life until I could put something together, for being an example to learn from. To my Aunt, for giving me my first taste of culture, for filling roles in our family when no one knew their lines. To my late Grandmother, for being what held us together, for creating a family that reaches across the globe, I write to fill the hole your death left in me. Much love to you all.

To the seekers who find the truth. To Holly Tharp, for being a fountain of grace when it was needed, for being a voice of comfort, for being a muse to the muse-less, for listening to the rain. To Josh Kent, for diving deeper into what it meant to be alive than I was willing to go at the time, for bouncing back thoughts others only dropped, for being the first to take the big steps. To Chaz Owen, for the willingness to grow when others said it was impossible, for never stopping, for carrying on the light that is bigger than us. To Colin Stahl, for taking it all seriously, for integration with life, for spreading the truth. To Melissa Kotter, for embracing and becoming, for accepting the adventure. To Zaq Kickasola, for helping build the foundation, for teaching to those who need. To the many other students who give and take the glory within us, you know who you are. Much Love to you all.

To Toney Little, a brilliant artist and musician. Many thanks for the cover art and for the words of motivation. Anything I may do to help your art, I will. Much Love.

To Et Cetera Coffeehouse, for providing us a place to grow for all these years, for being the location where I have meet the greater sum of cherished people, for being a home for inspiration. Much Love.

To my Truest friends. To Aaron Brian, oldest friend, a man who has never wronged me, a bright heart and a wise soul. To Macon Tucker, perpetual cell-mate, fellow magician in this machine, a true artist and a glorious mind. To Walter Pfeifer-Thompson, a man that has given more food, money, shelter, and energy to others than was ever expected, an honest ally who has provided sanctuary to our kind for a decade. To Brittani Harrington, steadfast in the storm of life, definition of beauty, bet you didn't expect to see your name here. To Thomas Dean Stewart, my best friend, sharer of the glory, co-creator of all I find pride in. There is little I can say to you four here, for it has already been said elsewhere. Regardless, you deserve more acknowledgment and recognition than I could offer. Much love to you all.

To Alan Moore and Peter Carroll. Please don't sue me for quoting you. That would be the least magical thing to do.

To the Gods, Muses, and Angels I believe in.

To Desaveh, and Artemis, and Orion, and Serazade, and Thoth, and Rahnmah.

To the Prophets.

To the Plants and the Worlds within them.

To The Source. All glory for you.

Forward

The cover of this book states that it contains work from 2006 to 2012. Though that is true, the essence of this book started in 2005 and continues well into 2014.

Nearly nine years of work has gone into this tiny little book that I feel a good portion of its readers will misunderstand. Nine years of capturing my growth through life on the page. Nine years of posting feelings online for people to listen to or mock. Nine years of standing behind the good end of the microphone. Nine years of gazing at the screen questioning my worth as the series of stanzas melt into nothing more than nonsensical sounds.

But now I am done, and I have something I can be proud of; and that is enough.

I've tried to publish this book 6 times now. Only one or two stanzas from that first childish attempt have aged well enough to show up in this collection and the rest aged like milk, and thus, were discarded. Regardless the essence has remanded the same from the conception.

This book is about listening. It is about ignoring what you have been told. It is about seeing that beauty of God; eyes open looking out or eyes closed looking in. It is about making things what they are not, and make the things that are not what they are. It is about the truth that can only be found in nonsense. It is about envisioning things within your mind like it was the cinema. It is about repeating gibberish until you truly understand what a word means. It is about asking the questions when you already heard the answers. It is about magic, more than anything, it is about magic.

The simple magic. The true magic.

That comes from observation of life and the realization that we are part of it, and it a part of us. Thus, the world outside you is a reflection of the world inside you, and you a reflection of it. Change comes from within. Effects to the pieces affect the whole. The Law of Sympathy.

And like all magical books, it lacks page numbers.

And when you find yourself not understanding a part of this cryptic little book, make something up. It will become true to you; and trickling through the subtle patterns of life it comes to be a part of me and you will finally understand what I mean.

.

Part 1- A Diner of Dreamcraft in the Blood

Our life is a complex twisting spiral in an endless blooming flower-bearing bush burning by the holy fire of God

The ones much larger than us gaze into our depths and find salvation

Our every action is a gyro-spherical twist of one or turn of another adding to this large composition we can call our own

***

The world becomes a coloring book

We all see the same picture

But we choose our own colors and that alone is enough to change everything

***

Our reality is ours to create when we realize perception and will are one and the same

The Catacombs are Breaking

There are three poems with this title that exist, and in truth, are part of a much larger poem. One is written by Samuel Hawkins, another by Christopher Williams. This one is by me.

We are dimmed lanterns looking for light.

We are the flash-bang in the hard-knock drum

beats; singing from flat-box guitars missing

strings. We are the pocket edition published

on the creative process' ten thousandth anniversary.

We are The Garden of Eden's lumber from all

those wigged out trees. We are children who got

much too competitive in full-contact make-believe.

We are both sides of the wall; we see all the green grass.

On one, we are making hammers. We are taking

trash, our repressed past, dubbed fireworks,

and our ex's toothbrush. We are taking and making

these things heavy. Like Adam, not yet knowing how

to dream, we are releasing our origami folding bones

for making handles for hammers. We are making a pride

of hammers. A canvas-load of hammers. A whole

congregation of homegrown half-human hammers.

On the other side, we are a choir of self-immolation.

We are the sound of forest fires. If fire was a song

it would be this. We are the buzz-drunk beat dropped

from Babel. We are prisms turning all wandering

through into light. We are the deafening silence

heard after the last loud note of the song called night.

We are so bright. There are not enough suns to be this bright.

We are hammers and suns and this wall is deflating.

These walls we post up around each other are falling.

There are so many souls overflowing with drowsiness

and it is well past early; best to wake them all up.

There are so many lanterns looking for light,

but thank God, we are so bright.

Beyond The In-between

Through the blessed overlap thoughts trust-fall upon me

as I sit like statues in a comfy chair by the window; filling

my mind's flask from the cascading colors and noise dripping

like a tap. I am desperately trying to catch something of worth.

I wish to take hold and watch it struggle, give up, struggle, repeat

and finally submit; pagestricken and mustang ready to break

me right back. The missing words wander through the attic

of my throat with grace that, until now, I assumed could

not exist. Even at my brightest, it's like treading through

water thickened with family. The grace stain takes form in

the invisible while spreading it's glowing arms and asking

"What's it going to be then?"

Here where inspiration stares back at us, and we are allowed

to reach into Calamity's orchard of "what-If's" and find something

of value. The voice opens itself like a concert piano and I play my

role without missing a key. Truth after stunning truth rushes around

and through me. Each blooming into a daydreamed masterpiece, with its own truths and perspectives to overlap and egregore this mind.

I'm overwhelmed. My cup overflowing and my hand ball and jacking

ever drop falling to the page; a burst of cryptographic inkblots thinning

out

like youth. Swollen and drowned I remember where and who I am,

and answer the question still tangled in reality like a doubt perched on a

prayer.

"What's it going to be then?"

Give me Everything. Give me nightmares, nightlights, and nights I'm left

wondering If there is more to see in reality. Give me grace, vitality, and

the mentality to make only truth; straight, bent or broken. Give me

courage

to make my words a spoken token left on stage. Give me rage. Give me

the

Hallelujah keys to open up the cage we put ourselves in. Give me saint

and

give me sin. Give me more to life than just some free-floating words and

a pen.

And the voice opens itself like a fissure birdcage and I walk within.

I've been in there ever since.

The Kiteflyer

Within the secret language of my soul there are many repeating themes; the most common of these being the kite. I have always related the kite to be like a spell or a prayer being sent off into the sky like a telephone to something bigger than us; or a casted line to bring down the sky fish. The flyer is, of course, you.

He ties another ribbon, The Kiteflyer,

one doubled knot on the tail for each retrieval;

half gift, half reminder that it was he,

he the one who pulled the kite down from the sky.

It was he who stuck the twine to its fragile framework

and taught it how to dive. It was he who wove the veins

to its skeleton to play teaching games with death.

He only uses the most beautiful fabrics.

Often he dreams of casting kites, the image comes to him

in mirages and figures. The chalkdust sky is the canvas

of a lover. These thoughts hum hymns and he feels the string

in his fingers, the skies pulses beating in his hands in perfect tempo.

He dreams in sanctuaries, but not in beds. He dreams of what is out

there unseen, unflown. He dreams of reeling in the lovely of the

invisible.

He flies only in storms; to feel the rain sink-holy to clean pores,

 feel the dazed electrics.

He goes through periods of fine-dined weather,

and in them he knows what it means

to be broken; sitting and twiddling the same stale ribbons between

thumbs.

There is so much not witnessed and he knows the waste of time,

blazed by the sunlight and mediocre.

He screams his prayers to pale blue sky. His prayers appear

in no hymnals, and thus, fall deaf to heaven. But when it storms

it really storms. And he flies, the string ringing unknowns

in his half open palms like an altar, the rain pounding its baptism.

And he gazes at the ribbons; his nocturnal rainbow in bloom;

each ribbon a story pulled from the sky, whispered by something up

there.

He thinks and somehow hopes the sky, with its moon and stars

and lightning bolts, feels jealous and breaks the kite string.

He thinks and somehow hopes the sky takes it back;

it's all half a gift anyways.

Pocket Words

This has gone through more drafts than anything I have worked on. It is the only poem I have ever finished.

Oh! What would they give,

        just to walk through the window;

to be somewhere else?

Two Moons

1.

Brightest,

stalled at idle

the seas and all that turns

within and without it realize

themselves;

silver

alone, just you

alone awaken all.

Unzip your midnight velvet. Turn

us as

a key

to a lock. When

the chambers of the world

behind things, now forever phased,

whisper

their click,

we will function.

Vibrant now like beating

hearts and loaded guns. Forever

guiding,

we all

turn just for you.

Inside myself, I'll hold

gently your form like it was the

last coin.

2.

I've watched,

night light noticed

the moon this darkening,

how it hangs, propped against the stars.

How it

resides

within the form

of a white citrus slice.

So sweet. So cold and wove with juice

our white

pearly

queen must taste here

tonight. Her light pours; pulp

and all. Every drop sinks deep in

our pores:

rivers

through the floodgates.

In her image we tilt,

our fruit in the sky. The night's an

orchard,

and us

the nocturnal

become the dark harvest.

How marvelous our brightest - wrapped

in peel,

and lace,

and white scandal -

lies close here next to us.

No sleep; lay awake together.

Her, smooth

and sweet

and clean. Us, worn

out and weary, finding

inside ourselves seeds to carry

and sow,

dropping

them here and there

for the daylight's others.

Wait for dawn's break, so we can plant,

sleep, dream.

Figure Drawing

The first time she modeled herself for me

was in the middle of a high dollar clothes

store, somewhere in the dusty pop- up book

of televised New York. It was early, 2 pm

or so, I had no coffee, pot, or cigarettes

and honestly, I had no business being

in a place like this. After hours of masquerading

in every article that fit her framework, we

left empty handed, minus a single piece

of chocolate. I didn't ask, but she read the wonder

from my eyes, saying she does this so she will

never forget how ridiculous she feels in those clothes;

buying charisma rather than the breath and purge

of actions and goodwill. With half the piece

of her overpriced chocolate unraveling

on my tongue, I began to paint a portrait of her

in my skull. A portrait of a bicycle, rider-less,

rolling downhill. She asked if she could keep it,

no one had ever captured her chain properly; the right

coats of dirt and rust. The second time she

modeled herself for me was in her friend's

cherry wood flat, somewhere near downtown Memphis.

We were playing cards alone by candle light after

the power went out like a blind boxer. I was half

nervous, twirling the cereal in my bowl like divination.

My iPod was humming its last drops to Cadillac Sky.

Until then, I had never seen anyone tap toes

to rain, never seen eyes outshine the lightning, never

had my ass handed to me in Egyptian Rat-screw

that badly. In her laughter, woven within my own, I tried

my hand at another portrait. Chandeliers this time, on yo-yo

strings, spinning around the room, brightening every

possible thing and then… Gone. As far as I know,

this piece still hangs above the mantle in her smile.

The third time she modeled herself for me,

she was laying on her stomach on top of my sofa

in Paducah, Kentucky. I was putting those college

classes to good use, capturing her form with as much

photographic grace the lenses of my fingers could handle.

The valleys of her shoulders, rain drops on her hips,

windowpanes in the shadows of her ribs. These things

are not metaphors, simply truths. Once she was reflected,

I rotated the canvas to show her herself

for the third time. I must have written my wonder

right back into her, because her eyes were tossing

question darts into my art. "What's a spine

doing in this piece? Why are there legs and hands

and hair? Teeth and eyes in a skin wrapped skull?

Is this me? Is this what people see?"

May she be,

always fireworks a moment before the bang. Always

those cracker-barrel horseshoe puzzles, and half a pack

of cigarettes shaped folded up like airplanes and flowers.

Always some part magic. I still have this unwanted

piece, somewhere, in some closet, in some folder,

tucked in tightly. I keep it there, so I can always

remember to forget to look at her like everyone else.

Prayer for Bohemia
This is stylized after a few Baha'i Prayers. Some of the lines are homages. Other are downright stolen; but it works with the flow of the poetic ideal of the Bohemia we long for.

In the name of the Lord, the Most Exalted, the Creator and Observer, the Dayspring of Inspiration.

In the name of the pen, and the ink, and the six word drenched napkins telling our story, The Lord who retired with a cup of much needed coffee, black, resting on the seventh.

In the name of The Almighty, The Brutally Merciful, the All Bountiful Tree with branches weighted and bowed, heavy of Oranges, Mangos, and Avocados,

with fruits foreign to earth, leaves of kiss-stealing shade, and bark ready to be deeply swayed into Campari.

I entreat thee, O my God, by Thy Most Great Names, whereby thou separated truth from denial, muse from insomniac madness, and verse from night terrors and shivering mumbling tongues, to send down upon me and my loved ones, those tired and chocking on their own voice, the illumination of this world and the next.

O God, O straight no-chaser God, O loaded pipe kite-high God, the Fountainhead of Revelation, the Author of all Bibles, Qurans, and Torahs, Author of the gospel in the chest, aid thy many artists to raise up the blessed and unending Word, which shines on the film in darkrooms, and can be read on Pollock canvases;

The Word which escapes birdcage pianos, and traces cursive proverbs in the cascading step work of dance; The word that can be heard vibrant on the fire-escapes of dawn, or the gridlock streets of midnight; The word of petitions, and prophets, and poets.

Healer in the Greatest Sky, your children closest to your image, blessed with your talent of creation cry out to you. The shallow breast of Bohemia, once filled with milk blazing and mad like Absinthe, have been drunk dry. Your blessed cry from the crib, Oh Lord, forsake them not.

O God, O blender of color and architect of stanza, aid thy servant to have a loving and tender heart, a mind open as the doors of an honest lover, and a tongue as tamed and sharp as a child, as to aid thy children of the streets.

My God, grant thy Artist these things, and I will spend my sunshine dreaming of you, and my moonlight worshiping your endless names. Thou art the Strong, the All-Wise, the painter of new colors, the choir of new octaves, the filmier of perfect film, the poet of finished poems.

Amen.

To Those Who don't Meet

his hands

very dry flowers

browning slowly

baking bread

black book phone

one number short

her hands

the waters

flowing more

her bland blood

lack of spice

two heartbeats

browning flower

damp filter

the last cigarette

Absconditus
From the Latin phrase Deus Absconditus, *meaning hidden or unknowable God. This poem is about hidden things.*

1.

He had practiced his eyes till illumination.

Running laps of sun cycles, conditioning in candles,

but not a thing could have readied him for the first time he saw

light; a mortar crack of curiosity.

2.

Facing

is a grocery term

meaning to straighten

and organize product on the self.

It's to give the impression that the customer is

in fact gazing into a solid wall.

Gaze three steps deeper though, and you'll

notice the calamity behind our perception.

3.

Do you ever feel like we've met before?

If a piece of us touched before our bodies did,

Somewhere before us?

4.

"I feel," I say,

"like my poems come from another plain.

And I have to reach through doors;

often like water, and often like broken glass."

He looks with unwishing eyes and says,

"Wait till the other door."

5.

Have you ever pondered why only

one side of the coin is lucky?

6.

I see myself in you.

I see my laughter in your eyes open,

my palms held doubt in your smile.

When you cry

your tears are my Amen's evacuation;

your make up runs fire-escapes I danced upon

once; I believe this.

We are made of the same stuff,

someone's sandcastle floating in daydreams.

7.

If reality is flat,

I'll half it like a dollar.

I'll let the eagle peck out the mason eye

and rest on your overlap.

We will rise like Mountains, and fall like Confetti.

8.

Bless me unknown.

Never let a day float forward

leaving me untouched.

Wash my mind of disbelief.

Let me know forever there is more

than they care to write hymns for.

9.

Beauty,

beauty is in the in-between.

Write your world on a chalkboard and blend your borders.

Skew the concrete outline leaving you in one dimension.

Be a prophet with but one truth.

Listen.

Now Listen harder.

Hear that?

If yes;

There is more.

If No;

There is more.

Whisperhenge

This poem is written in a traditional Anglo-Saxon style of poetry. This is a four beat Accentual verse with alliteration on three of the four beats and a Caesura pause; partly for tradition, partly so I could format this concrete space between the lines for subtly symbolism to the essence of the piece. To modernize it up, I added an internal slam style rhyme scheme... Just so you know...

In the passing on pathways

                                                I hear your poems.

In silent subways,

                                        hallways and sidewalks,

I hear you, pitching

                                        the humming your heart

sometimes trembles.

                                            Tossing the tongues

you delicately danced

                                            within the daily

noise like corner-girls

                                              casting coins,

wishfully wasting

                                          their evening wages

to the sea. But I hear

                                          the psalms you sing

rise alive

                                              like ledger lines.

Your unspoken spaces

                                        sporadic in placement

separates the seers

                                    from unbelievers. Secrets

are scattered between

                                        the bends and breaks

your soul sometimes

                                            make. Your sounds

pound pitches in

                                                places ears

refuse to hear.

like thunder. Though I	Ribcages rumble
is erased and replaced	try to escape, the thought
your verses volume.	by the need to raise
inside you. Speak	Amp up the voice
your mastery magically	in these spaces, spreading
someday, they'll listen	around you. Maybe
	to the secrets in silence too.

The Second Crash
Written for Thomas Dean Stewart

You'd like to think you were an egg benedict,

dropped out, all at once, from the clean cracked

shell of two tangled lovers in the form of a car crash.

Or that the whites would calcify a milky pearl around

a yoke of James Dean and some nameless innocents.

Or that some lips would meet yours; a second crash.

They'd taste something subtle and swallow; breaking you

down with her jaws of life; holding you inside curves

of skin and stories like the gospel inside a new hymnal.

But we are not eggs; at least not now, post womb.

And no country, song, or split legged waitress will

be enough beautiful wreckage to strip you from

a shell that was never yours. It's never enough to push you

to a complete mangle of complications and life, a birth,

Your second crash; there is just you to put you back

where you belong; in the eggshells of a tangled artist

with two hearts because one is not enough. With a soul

that inspires with the tale of its own beautiful car crash.

The Kites Inside Your Chest
Using all of the '20 Little Poetry Projects' by Jim Simmerman

My body is that kitchen drawer;

how the tools and toys inside

it sleep together without foreplay.

All things do this at some time:

allt losta og eru og skapandi.

Open it. Let your fingers to wrist

release textured parades. Glances

ricochet to shines from dulls. Nose

and teeth collecting spice-spliced dust.

All silent until strings are pulled, keys turned.

My body collects things it's lost.

They feel as soft as the overture.

We are all godly junkyards.

Sometimes Nervous like Nietzsche

in Jerusalem. But a week from now

you'll witness your usefulness.

Trust me, but maybe you'll

never know your uses. Prometheus

even, on occasion, burns the truth.

It rains a lot less than it once did.

Open the drawers inside

yourselves and release

the kites inside your chest.

Let them razzle-dazzle the moonlight

and steal the stars psalms.

Swing like your childhood, like

your sweetheart's noose.

The stories are rare, and thus golden.

All rare things are precious metals.

The swift strings of everything twist

and weave under there four-sided gods.

He's full of something all right.

Them kites, they'll cut the sky down.

For My Father, Catcher of The Bigger Fish
Written For Ronald Taylor

My father always hangs up the phone like I forgot

his birthday, reluctantly; like he's testing out a joke

and I wasn't there to get it and laugh; like he's

being harassed by attackers and I forgot our

telephone secret safe word for such a situation.

He always keeps things autograph brief like I got

a line here pushing behind him to talk the world

with me, and Dad, some days I do. But I am working

from home because I found how to sell my mind so

I don't have a boss-man to dig in me like you're used to.

Dad, I really got all day to shoot the shit with you.

But you see my Dad isn't one for misusing time.

He is too busy breaking fault lines on the tangible

Ground inside his head and bringing it to reality;

Too busy transcribing house shaped prayers to

graph paper and reeling them up like a good catch

for the people to see; too busy tilling the field of

a better-future garden for his family. And I suppose

some part of him expects the same for me. You see,

Mommy wasn't human enough to care, so he was the

only one ripping open the trash bags of hand-me-down

habits and genetics. And as a kid reciting Nascar numbers

was like Hail Mary's and wearing a UK cap was a ruling

passed before my birth I was predestined to pick up.

But I'm not like you, Dad. I have yet to bring my dreams up

from the clay and pass them life. I have never thought it would

be nice to go fishing then went outside and dug a pond, built

a pleasant little dock off of it, then filled it with water and fish.

Me, I would have just kept daydreaming. I have never sketched

up, designed, and built a wraparound patio in two days, single

handedly; I never sketched up, designed and in two days single

handedly built anything. I have never sold a house and risked

everything to in the end, despite fraud, despite being robbed by

your best friend and a woman who tried to break you; despite banks taking just because they can, you still have the home you

always wanted; this home you built with your own two hands.

This home where in the concrete is carved my name, Tyler,

like I did a damn thing to deserve this. Many years from now,

it will be my name people will see and remember there. Dad,

I wish yours was there too. Because I am not like you, Dad,

I don't deserve any trophies. I still cast my lines into the dark

hoping for the big fish, the urban legends and grandpa stories.

I am still hoping for a world where love isn't put in a closet,

where money doesn't dictate happiness and possibility, and

and where my future daughter can walk alone without wondering

if she will come home in one piece. I want my future children

to have a better world. So if my hook is swallowed, let this

poem be the concrete, let you name be carved in the foundation

of my craft, Ronald Wayne Taylor, a father who can turn

a page into reality like holy origami. I hold on till the day where

my work becomes true. That day, Dad, when I can be just like you.

The Mini Revolt

picket signs and inverted burning flags hang

from broken toothpicks and paperclips bent like America's spine.

scattered spare change gaze menacingly at us with their heads up.

the unpaid attention has run rampant, and the fragile

has come to collect. be alarmed that the things

in your pockets are more then not enough.

they revolt.

those small and unnoticed

        left out and below eyesight standards

        cut but cunning, pushing down walls

        from step ladders

those wanderlusting for things simple

        so they themselves become too simple

        if there even is too simple

those boxing rears off from stilts of outdated shoe fashions

        glowing bright mini from pockets

       forgotten or stranded

       petitioning breakdowns

       with signatures singing solos

those gargoyle stuck on shelves or cubicles

       alone until their codependent others require a sleep

       looking broadly up as they fall

       grounded and are not retrieved

those who still get feed from maternal piping

those who's word fall below commas

       art beneath standardized brushstrokes

       dancing under feet

       deemed so low that they are given away

       after dinner mints

those with records and books and films that can't best-sell on the shelves

       who drink alone drowned

       in pick-up lines and pleasant conversation

       that can and do retreat to the corners of the calendar

    forgotten x's of yesterday

those only large when wearing mask kept in wallets

    who's tall spiked heads

    long hanging legs

    are dwarfed by fearful censor whiteout

    shrinking in the shadows

    of father's failing plans of success

    or moral warfare WMD's

those whose hearts are suffocating

    their hearts simply can't fit

    their hearts simply can't

And I, with my toys and word-wise, with my hopes abounding, am joining the larger army.

Nine Days

For Ayat Al-Ghormezi; Inspired by her story

"We are the people who will kill humiliation and assassinate misery. We are the people who will destroy injustice."- Ayat Al-Ghormezi

She was taken up from her parents

house. Guilty for attempting to sow

hearts and minds with action & prayer.

.

I wonder if she tasted the smoke,

dust and rubble on her trembling lips.

Did every pause feel like a bullet

.

was stitched in her skull? Was every breath

a rush of psalms and adrenalin?

Did she bump up tempo for fear she'd

.

be cut short by sniper cliffhangers?

Did she present her work in the lost

tongues of her fathers and her mothers?

.

They pulled from her answers to their dull

questions. Who paid you? Why do you hate

your country? But all they drew was songs.

.

They wanted to know why she was so

bitter, but they dare not taste. Busted

lips dripped juice so sweet. They could have drunk

.

her dry, but they let her songs sing out

to the floor, forming thick dark rivers

of unread calligraphy. One word,

.

repeated over and over and

again, until the smooth strokes became

hypnotic. Justice. Justice. Justice.

.

It's not about Shia or Sunni,

but liberty. You can take the coin,

break down the podiums in pearl square,

.

but you can never kill a living

soul, and it only takes the actions

of one to rekindle an idea.

I ask, what is the price of a poem?

How powerful can hope be to the

senses of ones who stop and listen?

.

The screams of thousands fall deaf to the

ears of the unjust; the slow motion

deflation of stone walls is unseen.

.

Yet in the palms of a poet they

feel a pen through the waste in their hands.

Their ears hear hope through death and rape threats.

.

In their mouth they taste blood of the lost

through the spit shot there by prison guards.

Their skin feels laid hands through the beatings.

.

She could see it clear through the blindfold;

princess, tyrant. With every baton

crack, her eyes flooded with white static,

but still she saw it clear as daylight.

They couldn't change the channel. Her eyes,

were so in tuned. It took them nine days.

.

Nine days of beating all they could out

of her. They wanted to know what made

her tick in that time-bomb like fashion.

.

It took nine days. Nine days to breakdown

the world God built in six. When they were

done with her, all that was left was words.

Dandelions

ten thousand unshattered

pristine dandelions

tall shading

life below

districts of ankle-scrappers

whitewashing vast flat meadow

one grand gust proposal

dance of every seed lifting

blizzard in the spring

one unfulfilled wish-dipped snowball

distant intangible form

one million seeds seep

stretched woven twine

tangles of dreams

meadows littered

one million seeds

reblooming weeds

one million unshattered

pristine dandelions

stand tall

whitewashing vast flat meadow

closer

        still now

closer

Part 2- A Museum of Muse in The Heart

There is a common essence that is shared between many forces and ideas that we as humans find ourselves desiring and gravitating towards

It can be felt through passion and seen through beauty and expresses through charity and grace on top of a fountain of other things

It is bigger than good and stronger than love and is more useful than truth or freedom

***

It is a hard thing to place a finger on

but like a clock telling time if we listen it causes us to serve our truest function and the function of a writer is in the end simply to write and that is just what I did

***

The Muse who provides the inspiration for these poems should not be thought of as a girl nor a series of girls nor the moments of pleasure I shared with them

But rather one transcendental figure represented in a cosmic reflection of multiple moments with multiple women

In this world and in others

Heading Home

Written for Holly Tharp

I will never forget your eyes when I said

leaving is the only thing I ever believed I was

any good at; that the years of racking up

lines in Tetris came from suitcase feng shui;

that my scotch smooth word-wise and

desire to express like this is the cognitive

trickle-down of early morning apology note

footprints to lead my past off my trail;

that "you never know what you got until it's gone"

was the only way I knew to keep inventory;

I promise, I'll never forget your eyes. Those

fogged glass irises proving me a fool again,

like a lover perched under the front-porch light

not even having to yell a name to the dark.

Rib & A Smile

I fell into sleep on your floor an hour before you did. My head stone-dizzy from love life small talk, and that strange music you listen to now days paraded in high volume. My lips had a pleasant aftertaste, but I was still speaking of that drink which is somewhat sweeter.

I don't remember what was dreamed but I remember dreaming, and that I felt deeper in it than any lullaby had ever dropped from its bough.
Sedated by hopeful potential images, it was rearrange who found me awake.

We were all in a race to amplify everything. I was feeling pretty good about it too, till morning came, and I found myself cut open with things missing; and with what would become the poet who now sleeps on my floor.

My side was stitch up with ease; when you do what we do, you get good at putting yourself back together. However, I managed myself missing a rib, one who by fruit learned to walk alone, and who now sleeps inside of another.

I could try to take her, but of all the titles I hold a thief was never one and
I know I shouldn't be one now. It is then that smile walks by who calls my name,
and the mirror of my body make me question what pieces I will fill myself with.

And now, I find myself with a choice.

If you weren't what you are

If you were a memory, you would be one

we overlooked at the time, one we kick

ourselves around for, years later, because

a camera or film is something we left behind.

If you were a radio station, all the songs

would be sung in some weird fictional

language; with homemade instruments

keeping melody. Your commercials

are the most interesting thing on the air.

You keep me breathing these sounds.

If you were guitar strings, you would break

in the middle of a popular song, but the band,

in rock & roll fury, would keep playing. Later,

they'd turn you into bracelets we can't take off.

If you were a cupboard, you'd be filled with clothes

belonging to an old gypsy couple, scarves and hats

and coats, pockets loaded with songs and stories,

poems, knickknacks and dollars of gathered change.

If you were Ice Cream, you would be so delicious.

If you were a conversation, you'd be a collect call to
a suicide hotline, for small talk and a wish good night.

If you were a novel, everyone would read you, students
would write 35 page papers on the fluidity of your themes
and your ambiguous Kafkaesque end, but no one would get it.

If you were a card game, you would be made up on the fly
every time you're played, and people with broken poker-faces
would leave houses drunk and filled with chips and pretzels;
pondering deeply on their empty wallets, wonder where
the Money went when no one won a single hand of you.

If you were a stoplight, you'd be a slow stoplight.
All that came to your four-way alter would have
to stop their rushing, relax, and look at the stars.
If you were Israel, I would be Palestine.

If you were the ocean we'd all be wet.

If you were the sky we'd all feel small.

If you were a poem, you wouldn't have been written by me.

Two Cups
I started writing this poem in my head after I saw two people holding hands on my way to class one day. I ended up taking a sculpting class with them many months later, and they sculpted two cups.

They were, at the end of their wrist, what poems are written for.

Their fingers conceived a strange precision like gospel; fitting

and filling those openings with honest touch; crossing for lies was lost.

My eyes caught in the grasp of their held hands, I endured what I had

missed.

Every touch I'd ever shared was never an experience of home. Just

knowledge of another pulse; another proof that I wasn't alone. Their

fingers

always felt funny next to mine, like teenager cars not properly parked.

Every one-sided bound has since been released, now the only beat I feel

is what's ticking

between my own veins. Some nights it's hardly enough rhythm to keep

marching on. But I swear,

music must be all these entangled two know. Melodies seem to ring from

them head to toe.

Today their station's playing boxcar blues heard from uncharted trains

heading nowhere.

You'll see sound waves in their smiles; wine red canvas stretched lips, waiting for the sweet caress.

Such canvas is hard to find, and it reminds me my hands keep holding counterfeits;

filled to the brim with languishing bibles of poems and notes, trust me, they're preoccupied.

I find myself full on impressions rather than knowing the truth. Words are my forum

so I attempt to bring everything in to it, often disregarding my heart is sold to an imprint.

My life is more often lived in the binds of books than the world you will find them in.

In truth, I am simply two cups, one empty, one overflowing. Somewhere you're the same.

Let me pour into you and you do the same thing. Because I find myself, caught in

the reflection of two lovers who I try to mirror, but my hand instead is filled with poems, what ifs, dreams. Like two cups, one hopeful and empty, one hopeless

unless empty.

Somewhere out there is a lovely who's the same. There are many places

poetry should be,

the least of these is on paper. Fill me and I'll do the same, let us cast

aside our books

and let our words sleep inside the other. Maybe then, we can leave our

counterfeits behind.

Maybe then, people will write poems like this about us.

Three Triangles; or, How to Fall out of Love

1.

Apply pressure on the two triangle composition for Rewind. Force down with it the one triangle for Play. You should find little else to do with your hands, so using your lungs inhale the distortion that unravels.

2.

Keep in mind the player was simply built to sustain in its own fashion, thus all that is in motion is the act of working against current flow. Glimpses should be half caught and shouted as the tape backtracks. The air should be filled with racket, rattles, and ambiguity.

This is what you want.
This is what it sounds like.

3.

Ignore all notions to call this music.
Leave that to the children.

4.

Breathe deeply till it alone fills your lungs, the ears inside you

might hear some secrets that you missed before.

Any escape route hidden in streets of lyrics long memorized.

Stay on track. Don't you dare look away.

5.

We all have ways of hurting ourselves. Some are more creative.

Maybe try pushing the headphones in hard

until they bleed their noise within you.

Try piercing your heart if they left it tattooed,

or wrap your hands wrist deep in all the unread paper-cuts.

Remember this is all a remedy. You break to make them better.

As always.

6.

As the sound reaches the end amplify it to infinity,

and listen one last time to the story of what you were.

this time starting with the ending you had crafted unknowingly.

7.

Smile and start to sing along as you unlisten

to the many songs you at one time called your own.

Easter Eggs
This poem is better read aloud.

Every mark is a letter in a word.

Most you don't know how to read.

Every stain is a star in a masterpiece

you don't know how to see.

Every action an act in a play

where nothing is as it seems.

Every mumble a note in a song.

A song that you would sing.

                        And I'd sing along.

And I'd bring my dreams and they would ring a long like bells.

Forging perfect harmonies but you probably couldn't tell,

because my heart, I keep it suppressed. A ticking watch muffled

beneath this mess of things; but I fancy myself an artist

so I'm trying my best to express these things.

That's why you only hear me, in a poem.

That's why I only preach your beauty in a way where the words are

moving.

Soothing. Because I don't know many ways to say what I want to say.

So I hide it in here. Interwoven in every line are my hopes and fears.

Presented like Smoke Signals, Sibliminals, and Morse Code.

Like Inspiration puts me in Cipher mode and I unload while trying to relax

and let Syntax work for me but I can't help but feel uneasy.

Every mark a letter.

Every stain a star.

Every action an act,

Every mumble a song.

Every poem a balloon.

Enormous.

Filled to the brim with the lightest lights in reality.

Strung from my hands, I carry them with me.

And maybe someday they shall carry me away.

Leave for places unseen. Leave my Silence here to stay.

And maybe then I won't need a pen.

Opened with a blaze, you'll gaze deep within.

And maybe I won't need to hide everything in verse

because in reality obsessions are a lot like a curse.

When these balloons take me away

and I finally find my home

I'll reach in and say I love you.

And I won't have to hide it in a God Damn poem.

Alert

my heart strings are stretched and taunt

thick elastic vines sprouting from my chest

crimson radio-waves

back to home

where my heart is

with you

sometimes they get in the way

my friends pushing past them

to look out the windows

as if our car wasn't cramped enough

maybe it's adhesion plays part

in our pour gas mileage

I don't mind much

I'm just patient sharp broadcasting

even now my heartbeat

screeches an interrupting tone

maybe you're at your house

reading some heavy book

maybe you're washing dishes

or on the phone

or in deep sleep

it doesn't matter

drop everything

turn it up

listen

this is an alert

love

an urgency

these chambers and speakers are telling you

of the one it's other end is searching for

the one it has that it is missing

A Quiltstitch Waltz

1.

If you gifted me a piece of paper big enough to write everything;

every thought, every color, shape, sound, flower, bird, poem,

at the very end you'd find losing you, it's the last thing I want to

think about or do

                but I do still.

Examine thorough. You'll see that it's a treasure map.

Roll it up like a looking-glass and gaze through, see my

eyes gazing back at you; reflecting purer than mirrors.

see your soul. And the treasured X I laid on it.

Gaze clearer then crystal but skewed like cross-eyes,

cross my eyes like stricken boxer targets.

                                    Target Me.

My heart is a dandelion;

break it and it blooms 1000 times over.

Submerging fields in starlight parades.

Every flower, every seed, humming a note of the melody

played in your name. The overwhelming left my ears numb

but with your heartbeat, banging transcendent drums ascending

to heavenly choirs, left me reconciled in various extremes of silence.

I'm a walking psalm; my memories are my lyrics.

Your stricken in them. They flow like lost streams

and pulse like speeding cars. Sing tours in me.

My life, is a network of train-tracks that I walk,

balancing, on the edges, waiting for the engine to hit

and take me with it to whatever is coming up, whatever is

pride, and comfort, and not this. Will you wait with me?

Together, we are a dancing cataclysm, our bodies

and that which flows in and between them cascades

against walls we left standing. We break their angles

like wishbones and drink the marrow; tender calcium

whitewashes reality to blank pages.

                                               Let us write it all ourselves.

2.

Now, the thought of you chills my hands like ice. What if

we are snowflakes, taking simple pleasures to new places.

We craft strangers and projectiles or keep ourselves encased,

but we always starstrike with yuletide revelations and we always

leave the imprints of angels.

                                      What Graffiti did I leave on you?

3.

You are a quiltstitch. You are a waltz.

Your patterns,

                they are already foretold.

Chantepleure
Chantepleure is a dead English word meaning to cry and sing at the same time.

The old walls carry Graffiti in their palms and their pockets.

Some tags they packed up when they left home,

some they picked up like trails of bread and marbles of glass

as they try walking their way back.

Both are coins palmed for an eternal sleight of hand,

but the walls question how much was worth the cost

as they view their velveteen acquaint itself

with skin not of its own.

Serpent weaved tags twist together,

meta-merging into one harmonious discord

ringing existence proclamations.

Their voice hum a warm scarf of scars.

Being a man of colors and poise,

I tried a little Graffiti of my own;

tracing you silhouette like a picture frame

so we'll know you are intended as artwork.

Your figure was an open book,

I was hanging to its gentleness

like a Whisperhenge. But your verses

were unfinished so I wove in mine.

The images I laid on your palms, your fingers;

they were gloves to keep you warm. In them

you wore my heart, so when you held it

to yours you'd see them reflect.

The Images on your soles were bright notes.

Lanterns to leave your lyrical feet

candledriven to the melody of home.

Something neither of us ever knew.

And I had the Graffiti of my words,

the boldest thing I own,

my voice to wash you phantom ears,

cover the sounds you wish you'd never heard.

But the ink you let me stain your skin with faded.

It beats in your veins like morphine pianos,

humming ivory vibrations in your pulse,

but even blood is weaker than your walls.

Some things simply cannot and never will be unwritten.

All I wanted to do was reinvent your Graffiti,

but those old walls still stand like gospel choirs.

Their voices flowing in the night,

till you can't tell if they weep or if they sing.

The Orange

The orange was an engine found in a short dress.

Her fingernails were painted like caution, and so,

she unraveled the fruit as if it were dead sea scrolls,

and the lost gospel inside might bite her back.

I wanted to have her tenderness planted in my fingertips,

but I got her lips and I didn't complain.

I tasted zest, and flesh, and sweet. Peeling

the skin to see the hidden words within,

I no longer told the two apart.

The New Exhibit

Fossils of her are strolled throughout my house.

The fumes of our abrupt separation commandeer the air,

from where I painted these walls with memories & intentions

in hopes to fill my arms with something solid when we were

empty of each other. And yeah, I kind of need to pick a new color.

The whole thing feels like the new exhibition

in the "I told you so" Museum. Where comrades

storm the field from the sidelines, throat loaded

with cheap-shots, piping in hindsight, as they stroll

these rooms like a viper. Tracing a tangled timeline

from artifact to artifact, sticky note tongues posting criticism

like a caged dog, now free, to piss wherever it lands.

But the real treasure lies in front of me. The six page letter

sealed with a kiss, on which, I kept my promise. One last poem,

which with work, became this one. I burned those page, rubbed the

ashes to my lips, and felt the last warm touch you would ever give me.

Letter to Stranger

Lovely,

If you see me in the street or pondering on a bench I hope that my half smile and bright eyes will be enough for you to approach me and feel warm. It's rather a shame that we have yet to trade numbers, or eat together half sober at hours unknown to children and diligent students.

I'm sure I've seen you, somewhere, walking alone or perhaps holding the hand of your lover. I'll make more of an effort to talk to you in my own broken manor; which skips the tollbooths of small talk to get straight to actual conversation. Who really cares about the weather anyway? It rains sometimes, which is beautiful. That's all you need to know.

And maybe my prophetic abstracts are playing part now and I'll meet you in the rain without an umbrella, and we'll enjoy the sky-water and the awkward sprints of middle-aged women who attempt to not get wet. They always do anyways and it's quite funny. Come next storm I'll keep my eyes out for you.

Perhaps your hair will be red like the bright in exit or stop signs and I'll know my search ends here.

Dream Easy,

Griggori

Concretes
There is a poem in this book called Abstracts, which is a song of hope. This poem is not, hence the name.

1.

Her lips tasted like honey or regret.

I'm not certain which was stronger

but I'm sure of the aftertaste. It left

me speechless, her kiss ripped the

words right out of me. Without that,

I deflated with similarities to a balloon.

It always ended like this, left me asking

why we all kept coming back.

2.

My thoughts, they run circuits. Always going

and coming like the boomerang soles of lost women.

Maybe they feel like they're forgetting something,

racing to locked doors and searching for their keys.

3.

I'll hit you up when I'm doomed to return, I swear it.

4.

How deep do your footprints have to be before you

find yourself falling back in them? Are these man shaped

impressions in the bed sheets fossils of your nightmares?

Love, does laying with libraries let you get much sleep?

5.

Her lips were sweet. I'd close my eyes and wonder what all

else I was tasting. I'd lick my lips later and know many things

were left here. If I could skip time I know I'd see myself here again.

Maybe I'm just a quiltstitch too. I'd taste her lips and wonder why

it was never you. Oh God, It was always you.

Ledger Lines
This poem is the hybrid of three poems written over a five year period.

She rests, waiting on the rails. Nightlight green

eyes echo the city beneath her, yet still she feels

cast in its shadow; dark like midnight with her eyes

closed, dark like her hair caught on the wind's line.

And tonight,

                tempest.

She feels racket in her bones as the snowflake zephyrs

roll over what's still naked; uncharted legs meet the turn

of similar ankles and to feet, bare arms meet hand unheld

and bare neck meets lips unkissed. Wrapped only in the dress,

the dress as subtle as mutual longing; so bright, and so foreign,

she thought herself invisible, consumed by its slots for lust.

She once walked within me. My melody preconditioned in her footsteps,

barefoot, so the earth felt like it was stepping back, and they were equals.

Even so, she kept allegro like high heel traffic. Her figure, in metronome

sway.

She was the dazzler. The one who could be so cosmically fucked

she'd come out clean. The third and last starlight notch on Orion's Belt.

The girl so beautiful that when she left in the morning, waking up

from her first billing dreams, even the hearts of the Gods were left

broken.

She sung everythings in her breath. Resonating these four walls with

vibrancy;

leaving visions painted through spectacles. She sings a curiosity, a

daydream,

and caution's graze. She sings passion and silence, but there is regret

in the ledger lines; an eternity could have been written

in the ground untouched. The things I left unsaid.

She is not a canvas. If she was it would

only be to cover the colors she can't wear,

the colors of the other women,

and she does so poorly.

Though you wouldn't know it from my words,

she is not in boldness. She preferred to dance in the borders, waiting to invert the casualty of those who rest.

But now, she rest on the rails.

The wind reels tighter, and she lets go of all she holds.

Falling, deeply, into the invisible.

It's a shame you know. No one, not even I, ever told her how beautiful she really was.

Contained

Smearing ink on skin.

Casual old ways exchange.

A slight unwanting.

Deep lines within palms.

The constant feign of dancing.

Interesting hats.

Swaying long skirt dress.

Sharp needs to fill the silence.

Off and on relief.

Pomegranate tea.

Damp filtered half-smoked kreteks.

A Magnolia.

Part 3- A Picturehouse of Promise in The Skull

We all have something we are reaching for regardless of if it is in our reach or not

We all have something we picture to get us through the things we cannot cease to see

A filter to make the world we believe we cannot control more bearable

We all feel as if we are special and the ones around us are all part of the machine

***

Within us is a promise more ancient than rainbows

***

This is your world to be whatever it is you are destined and designed to be

Your enthusiasm is the answer

Anatomy

In the thirteen inches between

my brain and my heart, possibly

stitched like fine ivy in the vines

of my throat of sleeping tastefully

under my tongue, is a tiny hallway

of tiny rooms composing collections

of the small, overlooked, and forgotten.

Those things not noticed because of our

giants.

Inside there is a room wet from rainwater hallelujahs

hand-crafted by the ones I've known who've ascended

only to take the place of angels. Their hearts were soft,

so spongy damp carpet covers up the hardwood floors.

And yeah, maybe Mamaw didn't go up in a flaming chariot,

but her wings outshine any rides, bitches, or bling anyone

has even dreamed to see. So those walls are painted dark

as to complement her light in case she's ever to arrive.

Adjacent is a room left red from holding the ping-ponged heat passed between feet under blankets I've shared. One of us always wanted more, but didn't want to haggle on the price. So we window-shopped hearts, heads, and between legs before settling for something we couldn't see, just felt, because that's what we could understand. So I made curtains of blown kisses caught and hung them crooked and misplaced like scatter-shots because it's weird. And the ones I've stolen heat from would probably like that.

Two down is a room you might have heard outside because it hides every handclap and joyful noise I've got. It took a while to make a space worth having, but I remember every sound that echoes out. Mirrored from the door is a thumb-tacked blank page that might someday hold a masterpiece to catch the eye of passerbys. Maybe it can advert them from the floor's Dadaist origami and walls with holes that flood sight into rooms I've left blank for that reason. I'm hoping one day the pages will unfold with life to cover up some beautiful accidents with the words I held inside myself for fear that one day one of them might get out.

There is a room for holding hidden prayer,

for the last second of awe to a perfect song,

for the glowing lines traced in tai chi and

for the first times of the most amazing things.

And at the end of the hall is a locked door that I've never been behind.

It came that way. Every day I look for the key, under pennies on the ground

and the libraries in the irises of waitresses

and bohemians met on midnight strolls.

In every match strike and rolls of coins turned to a meal. I seek. I must know.

Every starlight that's stolen;

I must know.

Every smile;

I must know.

Every poem and word heard that shakes us and makes the giants less.

Until I find a ghost in the skeleton key that grants pardon to a room

holding

the tiniest of things. So perfect, it is hardly said to exist at all. It will

make

these great wall knocking our knees off track be like a jar dropped from

Jericho.

Everything will just seem still and quiet, and that which was heavy

 will be no more.

And in its shadow,

all I will feel

is small.

Thoughts While Watching a Dying Star

I hope you went out with a bang. I hope

that the lifeless planets dangling around you

like Boho-addicts drunk on your bright lightwine

were enlightened and consumed. I hope you

bloomed loud like a rose or bloomed red and wild

like the heart of the one who received it. I hope

the apathetic silence of space was deafened.

The choir of your heart sings the same flamestiched

tune as mine, star. We are not so much different.

You too shout into the crowed mountains of night

hoping to hear if your sentiments are echoed

or obtained. Let my souls' be your acoustics.

Know, star, I too am tethered to my mortality;

that tiny fast pinprick glistening in the distance.

Some nights, I feel it's so close I could grasp it,

and become just another dot fading into the perfect night.

Every Curve, Line, & Angle

My father paced the halls of this house

before he ever built it. Long before

the men in undersized overpriced

jackets told him it was theirs.

Every line, curve and angle

of counter-top and primed

but unpainted wall; every

submerged wire and pipe

and crumb in carpet; every

stain of ink, soda, and day

old soup lost in fibers; every

photograph adorning the walls,

coffee tables, and fridge; every

spice and backyard garden picked

meal wafting in your breath, every

laugh, every curse, every idea and rich

quick scheme echoing in our ears,

our mind,

our soul.

It was all there, dancing in his mind and rising

off memorized pages of graph paper

like a bewitched pop-up book.

He had it in him, and day by day

he laid down his legacy as it endlessly

unfolded like the marauder's map.

Them Birds

While walking back to my dorm from a class one night, upon leaving the building me and a group of equally lost students found ourselves walking into a blizzard of snow. We could barely see three feet in front of us. The ground was mighty slick, and the street lamps bruised everything into yellow shadows. About halfway back, what sounded like rockets going off echoed through the whole campus, further adding to the terror. I ended up walking a stranger back and staying in her dorm for an hour because we were quite terrified when no one told the students the day they decided to test the bird cannons. The whole thing was a beautiful frightening moment I'll never forget and it inspired this poem.

They're all so afraid of them birds.

See them birds fly way up to

the top of those tall buildings,

and the ones down here can't see

and it's got the ones down here

real spooked, see?

.

They been shooting rockets at

them birds; it gets them all real scared

so they scatter like a cup of

something that'd been knocked

over. Them ones that don't know must

of been real worried about them sounds

in the sky. Left you wondering 'who the hell

is killing us now?' Russians? Koreans?

Who knows?

Makes a man wonder. The songs are the birds but that don't stop us from singing them. And the sky is theirs too, but I'd be damned if we aren't up in it.

Damn shame is what it is. When we're done with them birds there won't be nothing left. Just feathers and bones tossed about, leaving you wondering what those things were for. And so then we'll go about looking for new things to spook us, new things to fire rockets at. New things to call ours.

Fire

The day you came back I had you name

sown into my right palm. I use that hand

for support like a tabernacle foundation

solid ground to grip as we hold what holds us

and draft their words like lottery. Everything

I do is in writing so you were the strong hand

pinning the pages as I work with my left.

You always were some kind of beacon or another,

glowing a path so I could tiptoe my pruning feet

into a field not my own. You were smooth like that,

and for a while you didn't know it. There are days

 I wish you never knew and we were still standing

on my back porch spinning dazzling what-ifs.

The day you came back you finish what you'd started

and started something else. There are days I still think

about those steps and the words spilled on them. "Go

ahead. I'll be fine." I learned to lie that day. I learned

I was pretty good at it too, and that there are

a lot more of those steps out there and you never know if your moving up or down. I guess that's just a part of I don't know, something.

Fly
Sometimes it is hard to read good poetry.

As I sit at my kitchen table,

the first place I have been able

to write this whole month long,

and start to read John Ashbery

for the first time, I repeatedly

catch myself distracted by a

clicking in blizzard staccato.

Above, a flying of the blurry

nature continuously strikes the

blades of a fan. He's not going

to die, I think to myself, as my

eyes trail words in the hallow

mock of reading we so often do.

There is no trap, no adhesion or

shock, nor poison nor crushing.

Only the constant slow bat-away

as it intends to reach the light,

flooding my ears with a river of wings.

There is much more poetry here

then you'd think, I think, turning

another page without reading it.

Armor

She said she's still looking for that knight in shining armor.

That particularly perfect dream-driven lover

that would never open curtains left closed, walk in and harm her.

She said never again would she go to another

child in a man size suit just playing hell-bent games trying to disarm her.

She promised me that. She promised herself that.

She use to say we were all wandering parts of a puzzle,

each flawless and unique. She said life was a great big puzzle,

an endless mosaic on the walls of all that we are. And aren't

we all just looking for a place to fall into, and rest peacefully.

That was my favorite part.

When she turned strangers to friends in her loving way she asked,

"Where do you fit it? What spectacles are you holding inside you?"

She'd state, "I am the petals of a blossom inside a starlight garden.

I am Venus' glistening goblet, overflowing with graceful aromas.

Artist mimic me on paper when they need something truly beautiful."

Sometimes, I just try to step back and see this fresco she spoke of,

But when I do, I don't see the grace she once had sketched in my mind.

There are no flowing stars of Vincent, or charming faces of Picasso.

There are no Seascapes with Lighthouses, or simple cabins in a summer meadow.

When I step back, I see floods of television static. I see fires, and I see prisons.

Where are the gardens? Where are the flowers?

She says, "I am a puzzle piece; three prongs and one cutaway. And I have been torn, bent, and broken. When you force things where they don't belong, the Images are distorted."

Her walls have been torn like Jericho, and she doesn't know the detrimental lurking soulless from those she calls her own.

She says she's looking for a knight in shining armor. But really, she's just looking for the Amour. She's tired of nights curled up tightly in bed sheets, hoping they'll turn to safe hard stone.

She's tired of feeling alone, without a home or someone to cry to.

I want to give her Amour like a picture frame. Something that will hold

her and say, *"This is what remains. But I know, if she'll let you this far,*

you will see that she is the most beautiful piece of art. Please, keep her

safe,

she doesn't need any more arrows straight through her heart."

When I step back and stare at this wall we've made,

I see perfect little girls ripped early from the womb of childhood.

I see a 20 year-old Bahraini poet, beaten till the blood from her lips

writes a poem they'll all agree with.

I see palms gripping prison bars, wet from tears of a woman's face;

facing life from trying to save her children's.

I see razors reflecting the face of an adolescent waiting

for any scrap of love like a lapdog.

I see the church choir gossip ping ponged back and forth and again

because they don't know the reason for the divorce.

I see daddy's little girl dancing her lives away,

answering to any name till she slowly forgets her own.

I see women slowly turned into stone

as they drift classification from person to object.

I see a women screaming "fire" till her lungs rupture

because you can't scream rape. No one will come for rape.

I see a forgotten baby girl, baptized in trash-bags,

a concluding kiss of duct-tape sealing   her lips.

The images are distorted. We're forcing things where they don't belong.

Stripped from our ribs was crafted the gift of dreams coursing of veins.

Yet we break it and bruise it like we are not part of the same thing.

Like our body isn't a house of cards that will collapse if we discard

an essential part and we're all just a machine spring-loaded to break

hearts.

She was supposed to be that center piece to catch the eyes of each who

pass by

She was loving and kind, And now she wonders

if she'll still see the stars in the sky.

If she'll hear the songs of birds like she used to. And every day is a

struggle

to pull her back to the world she's tried so hard to erase, and let her know

she's still loved; that there is life beyond the car wreck of pain and skin.

It is our duty. To rearrange the images we overlook every day.

Those wandering tortured puzzle pieces, be their armor.

So when the day comes, where our heavy feet stroll to a place of rest,

every flower is within its intended garden, every piece of the puzzle

is gathered to where it's blissfully aligned. So we'll all, women and men

alike,

We'll all have that perfect starlight garden to peacefully dream inside of.

Small Talk

Have you forgotten your stories?

Our tongues are soaked

with small talk and

bitter nothings.

Tell you verse.

As the last words

caught in your throat

beat a hum against

your teeth clasped

like church doors.

I will sing along.

Inviting the melody

caught in the people

to hold on to this song.

Tell your story

If only once,

so to return to your weather

and quiet what ifs.

You Should Let

The dots in your eyes condense until they transmute

themselves into the form of a flapper girl, soothsayer,

trapeze artist, or whatever you need to feed your interest.

She will whisper her mind to you :

Listen, your soul is a person shaped

guitar case filled up with birthday balloons.

Each one is a color you may have seen

but never quite heard like this. The case

has three locks, is buried under concrete

and is blessed by sage, holy water, & voodoo.

Listen, all of these balloons are being holiday

stuffed with air passed through pressed lips

casting new-holy hymns within their skins.

There is a million of them in there, babe, so

what do you plan to do with all of this pressure?

And all of this hits while you were cooking your eggs, or driving your car, or walking alone in the park, You will find yourself left wondering what you can do to exercise your soul of this air. What line you could write or idea you could invite or provider to reach straight through the surface and fill this world with a few new fresh breaths of what you keep within.

Abstracts

I once tried to publish the original 14 pieced version of this poem only to be told it was indeed good enough, just too long for their taste.

1.

Blinking red lights proclaim

a child is born at 4am.

7 pounds even. A majestic little girl

with ten fingers and ten toes

that have been counted

more times than the stars.

Her parents unexpectedly stumble

over a name and wrap her in a safe

blue blanket.

2.

The scream of a bullet echoes

off the two wall corners,

as a young man watches

his brother die for a color.

3.

Shades of azure

cloud to black, in the veins of

a woman pushing the needle

just a quarter inch deeper.

4.

Filth coins, 21,

and a folded piece of paper fall

in an old Yankees cap, on the side

of popular streets. Cliff notes

from an ever-growing love letter

revive the heart of a man who forgot

to hold sober and home.

5.

A garage resonates the chords

of a song no one will ever hear.

6.

A disciple of the lost art,

observing,

gives the time to notice that the pale lines

in the sky that follow a jet plane, are purest

when they exit their starting position,

and slowly erase into the chalkdust background.

7.

A small girl sings a psalm

between her hands, clumsily holding

each-other like unborn twins.

8.

Numbing purple paints

the stomach of a woman

as she begs him "Please,

just not my face." Keep

it covered, no one needs to know.

9.

Billy Collins stares

out a kitchen window.

10.

A tender kiss on the neck

of a girl makes her rethink

the self-deprecating words,

darkly scratched in pages

of her recycled five star notebook.

She covers her face in her messy hair

so they won't see her smile.

She's not use to feeling beautiful

and even less use to being opened by girls.

11.

Nails, big around as a diploma,

are forced below by the aching hands

of a man balancing mortgage and his

child's education.

12.

The tip of a sharpie leaves stunning murals

on the figure of an Artist's girlfriend.

You can see the fire in his eyes,

because he's never had

a clean canvas to work with.

13.

A young child watches two lovers

in subtle embrace, and he wishes for once,

just once,

someone could awaken the man inside him.

He takes a razor and carves into his wrist.

14.

Colors blend to perfect tones,

in the lost eyes of a man holding bars,

hearing the words "I forgive you,"

from the weary mouth of his victim's

brother.

15.

A new anthem rings around

the world from static stained

radios.

16.

5 dollars,

one composed of a quarter,

3 dimes,

7 nickels &

10 pennies,

all of which were wrapped

in spilled Dr. Pepper and cigarette ash,

find their way in an artificial wooden plate

and give a starving boy an apple.

17.

Clumsy hands wrap around

the palms of a boondocks angel

and for the first time

are led to a loving home.

18.

Blue skies mirror the veins in

a woman who learned to let go.

19.

The Artist explorers his canvas

in newer forms of intimacy.

20.

A man strikes gold

when his son finds

the lost cure.

21.

A woman unveils her beauty

to a man who can love her

without the bottle.

22.

3 pink words,

scars of a razor that was once

carved in the wrist of a long lost child,

reflect in the eyes of a powerful man

and remind him to always find beauty,

always pick the lovely,

and to smile.

23.

An observant messiah consumes

a beautiful poem about windows,

feels it tick inside him. Comes home,

and gives the time to write these words;

"Like chalkdust sky,

like scripture on coins,

like the colors in your eyes,

like colors in your blood,

like scars on skin and ink as well,

like notes locked tight and nails beneath them,

like pray in the night,

like names on birthpaper,

like your anthems and kites hidden in your chest,

beauty is in the in-betweens.

I don't know as much as I claim to know, or nearly what I'd like to but I try to. I watch-out for fast things and airplanes, and those that do the same. I listen to the words, even when they aren't spoken, but really that's nothing special. And I write. It's how I escape. It's how I express. It's not at all what I'm good at. A poet doesn't write. They watch. Words are just a way to get you to watch too, because there's a lot of good out there, just have to look a little closer. Life's a struggle, God we all know that, but when you can look up and see the airplanes overhead, Moving faster than anything, the line stays clean if you follow its guidance."

24.

Butterflies are chased

by a majestic Little Girl.

Emily. Her name is Emily.

It would have been Michael,

Peter, Paul, Jacob but things

don't always go as planned.

Her parents are aware of the meaning

because they grabbed it in a book.

It means to Excel, and really,

isn't that all what we are trying to do.

Un-Anchor the Angels

I like to fly with the angels. I like to feel my feathers

unclouded and spread wide; like the sky is the front

of my parent's fridge, and I'm that lone magnet

on a sea of white, holding up frames of happiness

and trying to tap into this heavenly electric connection.

And when I see her,

I know that she's the same. But somewhere shame

sprained her wings and she doesn't fly like she once did.

From these heights I see her walk with the people

like she's one of them. I can see she's too afraid to ever parade herself.

Best to stay on the shelf where she won't stand out.

Better to be missed than to be noticed by the wrong kind of eyes.

But her wings are hard to hide no matter what she stand behind.

I want to hear those songs she can sing from her light inside,

but her brightness doesn't penetrate the night anymore.

Not since someone penetrated it's way inside the doors of her soul.

So she turned down the volume of her gospel. The good news

that those magi and shepherds could use will have to wait until another

day.

Where are the queens? I don't want to be around the 3 kings alone.

I'd can fly, sure, but please someone just give me a ride home.

She feels alone.

Even though these streets are overflowing with the angels we've

forsaken.

Meanwhile we are shaking the hands of our societies twisted past

and somehow still have the pride to call ourselves men. There are

feathers

in the gutters; burnt bent quills from where we caste away

their records of defense. How many shots does it take

until it's not rape anymore? If we call her a whore does it make it okay?

How much weight does it take to hold an angel down,

to keep them here on the ground with us?

Please, you hidden angels, you shepherds and magi

and seekers following your glowing stars,

do not let the strings of your heart rust.

Let this night and these words be

the keys that release the locks

holding down your eyelids.

Maybe then, we can take the appropriate action to attack the problem

at its root. We must reconstruct the educational foundation of a nation

that

embraces watching its people break beneath the greedy grip of hate.

We must teach our sons that love is a two way interaction.

That it is sharp and it hurts because it is an offering and a sacrifice,

not because it's a knife. Like violins, and paintbrushes,

and a baby child, anything beautiful has a proper way of being held.

We must show them it is the humblest spark that burns through the night.

We must open the eyes of the ones we forgot and show them

they are not alone. This place is still your home

and we will clean your streets until they meet a higher standard.

Redemption is here. So no more tears, darling, no more fear of flying.

Tonight, we are regrowing our feathers.

Tonight, we are releasing the weight of these memories they hold up like lone magnets. We are replacing them with the beauty

of a better tomorrow. So no more sorrow.

Let your voices sing.

Because somewhere we allowed these cannibalistic less than men to stop

having to clip their wings. After fox news, NBC, and CNN

forgot which side to condemn, it became easy to brush off

an act from where there is no coming back. She had it coming.

What do you think those clothes are for? your egging us on.

It's like the songs say, I know you want me and I hate these blurred lines.

She had too many drinks. Isn't it a shame to see these two young men

lose their career like that? It's sounded more like a yes than a stop.

No, they don't have to clip the wings. The Media already

anchored them down. A magnet falling off the fridge

from holding on to the heavy images alone. If home

is where the heart is, than why is no one home right now?

So please, You shepherds and magi and hidden angels,

you hangers of photos and memories, and walkers of these streets,

please, un-anchor the angels. Allow grace like rain to cleanse

your every pore. Cleanse your eyes until you find that friend

who ponders the end and fill them with you hymns of life.

Cleanse your ears until you hear every cry and scream weaved

between suspicion-stitch tales secretly speaking of hell.

Cleanse you mouth until nothing cold and calloused comes out.

Cleanse your feet to lead you to act outside of these room

when this show and this night are just a memory in your life.

Cleanse your heart.

So we can start to fly. Instead of trying to hide our wings.

We can sing, instead of trying to rethink our gospel.

We can prosper. We can blossom and bloom.

We can release the weight of that hate and hold up beauty,

as were intended to.

Thoughts While Cooking Red-beans & Rice

1.

If emotions could be collected and condensed,

packaged and sold, which ocean would you submerge

your veins in to get yourself stoned?

2.

I once heard if you take two sports and hybrid their essence,

you're left in the end with a better sport; like magic, the product

is stronger than the sum of its parts. If this is true, I hope

bobsled jousting gets picked up by ESPN.

3.

I always related to and admired John the Baptist

more than Christ. And maybe that's my sin. Pushing

myself to keep getting lost in the forgotten wild cities,

to perform subtle miracles, to bring the bodies up for air.

4.

I want to tie-dye the moon, and whitewash wall-street.

5.

Always I notice you in the distance;

sunbeams surround and frame you,

your hair contorting in waves like neon

signs left off and dark; you beacon

in odd hours. I wait through thousand

hour nights for the mourning shift.

6.

If atheist truly believe that this is all that there is, then why

do they not have more hospitals? Why is no woman or man

being revived in "God is Dead" ICU, or being born in the birthing

wing of " This is all there is" Medical Center?

7.

I want to hold you like Braille.

Feel the patterns of your body

reflect in the suppressions of my fingertips.

Lovely, you are the only story I care to caress.

8.

What if my future son opens the door to my office hoping

to speak the burdens loose from his lungs? With Irises heavy

and wet he would unveil that he wants to be a Banker; that

he had known this his whole life despite dance lessons and

youth poetry slams; that new genetic research shows that

these traits are natural throughout the biosphere. Even with

a father's love, would this strike a wedge within our relationship?

9.

In a dream last night I was told that a Goddess I loved had taken

her own life? When a star of the divine divorces life it takes everything.

Even its existence. Even your memories. Now I'm left feeling lonely,

wondering what she was like, and realizing why my prayers felt so

empty.

10.

I wonder if our names

Are carved in the bullets already

Like a risky magic trick

I wonder if they tucked them

In the pockets of our clothes

To pick up our scents

11.

Maybe this needs more salt.

About the Author

Griggori Tyler Taylor is a writer, visual artist, performer and mystic based out of Paducah, KY. His work has been published in Word Riot, Toasted Cheese, and Notations. He is one of the founding members of The River Renaissance, and is a frequent performer in Paducah Writer's Group at Etcetera Coffeehouse.

:or,

Eldinazi Lycrii Vahnterri is a voice in your head; echoing lines of pristine senselessness until the pictures planted within your skull bloom as they always do. Take heed. Your time is now.

www.ingramcontent.com/pod-product-compliance
Lightning Source LLC
Chambersburg PA
CBHW020911090426
42736CB00008B/587